# Welcome to  xtb Issue One

## The Book of Beginnings

XTB stands for **eXplore The Bible**.

Read a bit of the Bible each day. Investigate the beginning of everything in the book of **Genesis**. Zoom in on **Matthew** and **Acts** to find out who Jesus is and why He came.

**Are you ready to explore the Bible? Fill in the bookmark...**

**...then turn over the page to start exploring with XTB!**

PROMISE

## Table Talk FOR FAMILIES

Look out for **Table Talk** — a book to help children and adults explore the Bible together. It can be used by:

- Families
- One adult with one child
- Children's leaders with their groups
- Any other way you want to try

Table Talk uses the same Bible passages as XTB so that they can be used together if wanted. You can buy Table Talk from your local Good Book Company website:
UK: www.thegoodbook.co.uk • North America: www.thegoodbook.com
Australia: www.thegoodbook.com.au • New Zealand: www.thegoodbook.co.nz

**Sometimes I'm called**

............................... (nickname)

**My birthday is**

.................................................

**My age is**

.................................................

**My favourite dinosaur is**

.................................................

| OLD TESTAMENT | NEW TESTAMENT |
|---|---|
| **Genesis** | **Matthew** |
| Exodus | Mark |
| Leviticus | Luke |
| Numbers | John |
| Deuteronomy | **Acts** |
| Joshua | Romans |
| Judges | 1 Corinthians |
| Ruth | 2 Corinthians |
| 1 Samuel | Galatians |
| 2 Samuel | Ephesians |
| 1 Kings | Philippians |
| 2 Kings | Colossians |
| 1 Chronicles | 1 Thessalonians |
| 2 Chronicles | 2 Thessalonians |
| Ezra | 1 Timothy |
| Nehemiah | 2 Timothy |
| Esther | Titus |
| Job | Philemon |
| Psalms | Hebrews |
| Proverbs | James |
| Ecclesiastes | 1 Peter |
| Song of Solomon | 2 Peter |
| Isaiah | 1 John |
| Jeremiah | 2 John |
| Lamentations | 3 John |
| Ezekiel | Jude |
| Daniel | Revelation |
| Hosea | |
| Joel | |
| Amos | |
| Obadiah | |
| Jonah | |
| Micah | |
| Nahum | |
| Habakkuk | |
| Zephaniah | |
| Haggai | |
| Zechariah | |
| Malachi | |

# How to find your way around the Bible...

Look out for the **READ** sign.
It tells you what Bible bit to read.

**READ**
Acts 1v1-5

So, if the notes say... READ Acts 1v1-5
...this means chapter 1 and verses 1 to 5
...and this is how you find it.

Use the **Contents** page in your Bible to find where Acts begins

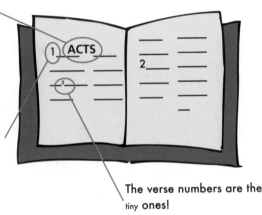

The chapter numbers are the **GREAT BIG** ones

The verse numbers are the tiny **ones!**

Oops! Keep getting lost?
**Cut out this bookmark and use it to keep your place.**

# How to use xtb

**1** Find a time and place when you can read the Bible each day.

**2** Get your Bible, a pencil and your XTB notes.

**3** Ask God to help you to understand what you read.

**4** Read today's XTB page and Bible bit.

**5** Pray about what you have read and learned.

**6** If you can, talk to an adult or a friend about what you've learned.

## Promise stickers

This copy of XTB comes with free **Promise** stickers.

We're going to explore three Bible books—Genesis, Matthew and Acts. We'll discover the same thing in all three of them—that God **always** keeps His promises.

*Be ready to stick in a Promise sticker every time you read about one of God's Promises.*

Are you ready to spot your first Promise? Then hurry on to Day 1.

# DAY 1 ACTION MEN

The Book of Acts

## DR. LUKE

ACTS is the second book written by a doctor called Luke. His first book (Luke's Gospel) tells the life of Jesus.

 Have you read any of Luke's Gospel?

Maybe you used **Christmas Unpacked** or **Easter Unscrambled** to help you.

## ACTION!

**ACTS** is short for "Acts of the Apostles". It's all about how the disciples (now called apostles) began to spread the good news about Jesus.

Their main **ACT** was to tell people all about Jesus. They were real **ACTion men!**

## NICKNAMES

Do you have a nickname?

What is it? _____

**ACTS** tells us about the first followers of Jesus. They believed that Jesus was the **Christ** (*God's chosen King*), so they were given a nickname—**Christians**. People who follow Jesus are still called Christians today.

## CHATTERBOXES

 Are you a chatterbox?

A chatterbox **can't** stop talking. The first Christians couldn't stop talking about **Jesus**.

Look out for the **chatterboxes** as you read ACTS. *Start now on the next page.*

# THE NEVER ENDING STORY

Acts 1v1-5

**Spot the difference.** There are eight to find.

Luke's first book is the life of Jesus.

His second book tells us what happened after Jesus died and came back to life...

## READ
### Acts 1v1-5

What did Jesus tell His followers to wait for?

> **Wait for the g_____ my F_____**
> **p_____ (v4)**

The apostles are going to be telling people about Jesus. They're to be **chatterboxes**!
And they'll get into BIG trouble as a result!

Jesus knew they needed help. God the Father promised to send them a gift—a **Helper**. Who was the Helper? (v5)

> **The H _ _ _    S _ _ _ _ _ _**

*Stick a Promise sticker here* ➡

**THINK + PRAY**

The Holy Spirit isn't a force (like electricity). He's a **person**. He's **God**! He helped the apostles to keep following Jesus—and to tell others about Him. Following Jesus can be difficult sometimes. We need help too. Ask God to help you—even when it's hard.

# DAY 2 MISSION IMPOSSIBLE?

Jesus has spent 40 days with His followers. But now He's going to leave them...

## READ
### Acts 1v9-11

What did the two angels say?

> Jesus has been taken into heaven. But He will
>
> c_____ b_____ (v11)

The disciples seem to be on their own—but they're not! God is going to send them the Holy Spirit. Read what Jesus said the Holy Spirit would help them to do.

## READ
### Acts 1v8

Can you read backwards?

The places on the map are written in **mirror writing**. Can you read them? (If you're stuck, a mirror will help.)

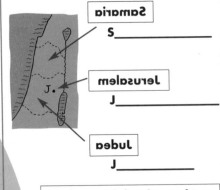

Samaria

S_____

Jerusalem

J_____

Judea

J_____

The ends of the earth

The e_____ of the e_____

*Check your answers in v8.*

*The disciples were to talk about Jesus in all these places!*

It seemed an **impossible mission**. A bunch of ordinary men telling the whole world about Jesus. But the Holy Spirit helped them to do it!

**Where do YOU live?**

**Try writing it in mirror writing!**

## THINK + PRAY

The news about Jesus has spread far beyond Jerusalem and Israel. It has reached **you** and **me** as well. Who tells **you** about Jesus? _____ Ask God to help them.

# DAY 3 THE CHATTERBOX TEAM

**How many correct chatterboxes** (like this  and like this ) **are hidden in the box?** _____

*Check your answer at the bottom of the page.*

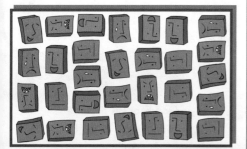

The disciples (now called apostles) are leaders of the ACTion team who would take the great news about Jesus to the whole world. A kind of **Chatterbox Team!** But there's a problem...

...One of them is missing!

There used to be **12** disciples—but one of them turned his back on Jesus—and helped Jesus' enemies instead.

Do you know his name?
**J_____**
*Check Luke 22v48 if you're not sure.*

Now it's time for the other apostles to fill the gap. What kind of person do they need? (*Choose from the list*)

Knew Jesus
Strong and brave
Clever
Good at making speeches
Liked cream cakes
Good at football
Follower of Jesus

**Check what Peter said...**

**READ Acts 1v21-26**

**Who was chosen?**
M_____ (v26)

Matthias didn't have to be clever, or good at speeches. He had been **with Jesus** from the beginning. Now the **Holy Spirit** would help him to be an apostle, an **ACTion man**—helping others to follow Jesus and tell the world about Jesus.

**THINK + PRAY**

Jesus wants the whole world to know about Him. Who do you know who tells other people about Jesus?
_____
(*In your church, or school? In another country?*) Ask God to help them.

**Answer:** Well done if you spotted all eleven!

# DAY 4 GREAT TONGUES OF FIRE!

Match each flag to its country and language. *One is done for you.*

UNITED KINGDOM

SPAIN

FRANCE

GERMANY

**Le Seigneur soit loué!**

**Praise the Lord!**

**Lob den Herrn!**

**El Señor sea glorificado!**

The puzzle says "Praise the Lord!" in four languages. In today's story, people praised God in **loads** of languages that they had **never learned**!

→ **READ**
**Acts 2v1-4**

God kept His promise to send the Holy Spirit. What **three strange things** happened? *Draw (or write) your answers in the boxes.*

| Verse 2 | Verse 3 | Verse 4 |
|---------|---------|---------|
|         |         |         |

**THINK SPOT**

How will these new languages help Jesus' followers to be chatterboxes about Him?

God kept His promise to send the gift of the Holy Spirit.

**THINK + PRAY**

Stick a promise sticker here.

PROMISE

Thank God for always keeping His promises.

# LOOK WHO'S TALKING

It was the day of **Pentecost**—a Jewish harvest festival—so there were loads of people in Jerusalem for the celebrations. *Use the arrow code to find some of the places they came from.*

**Arrow Code**

A= ⇧
C= ⇨
D= ⇘
E= ⇩
G= ⇦
I= ⬆
K= ➡
L= ⬊
N= ⬋
O= ⬅
P= ⬊
R= ◁
T= ◁
U= ▽
Y= ▽

Who made sure these people were there at the right time?

⇦ ⬅ ⇖
___ ___ ___

God wants the whole world to hear about Jesus—so He brought people from **huge** distances, and gave the apostles all the **right languages** to speak in! **Brilliant!**

But not everyone listened. Some people laughed and

⇘ ◁ ▽ ⬋ ➡

said they were ___ ___ ___ ___ ___ (v13)

*More about that tomorrow.*

⬆ △ ⇧ ⬋ ▽
___ ___ ___ ___ ___

△ ▽ ◁ ➡ ⇩ ▽
___ ___ ___ ___ ___ ___

⇨ ◁ ⇩ △ ⇩
___ ___ ___ ___ ___

⇩ ⇦ ▽ ⬋ △
___ ___ ___ ___ ___

## READ
### Acts 2v5-8

Some of these people had come a **H-U-G-E** distance. Travelling from Rome to Jerusalem is like walking from Land's End to John O'Groats or Sydney to Adelaide or New York to Chicago — **TWICE!**

## THINK + PRAY

Have you been to any of the countries on the map? _____
The message about Jesus has spread **much further** than that. It's reached the whole world—including **you and me!** Thank God for the people who tell you about Jesus. Pray for anyone you know who teaches about Jesus in another country.

# DAY 6 PETER PIPES UP

The apostles have been accused of being drunk—but Peter says **not**! *Take the first letter of each picture to work out these key words from his speech.*

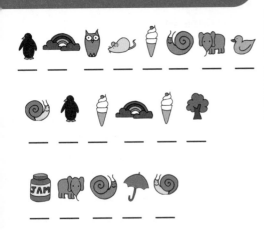

Now use those words to find out the main things Peter said in his speech. *Fill in the gaps.*

God P_____ long ago that amazing things would happen when He poured out His S_____. It was always God's plan that J_____ would be killed—but God brought Him back to life again!
J_____ is the promised C_____, and is ruling as King in heaven. Now He has poured out His S_____ on His followers.

Now read how Peter ended his speech...

## READ
### Acts 2v36

Acts 2v14-36

*Use v36 to fill in the gaps.*

God has made this J_____, whom you crucified, both L_____ and C_____

**WOW!**

Peter told them that Jesus was the **promised King**—who came to **save** them—but they **killed Him!**

**Stick a Promise sticker here** →

PROMISE

**THINK + PRAY**

We'll find out tomorrow how the people reacted to Peter's news about Jesus. Are **you** thankful that God kept His promise to send Jesus? **Why**? Talk to God about your answer.

# DAY 7 — WHAT SHALL WE DO?

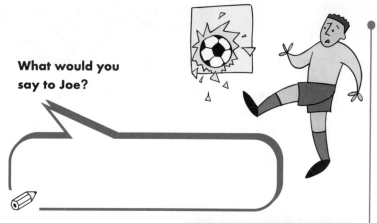

**What would you say to Joe?**

Peter says they must **turn away** from their sins (repent) and **turn towards** Jesus. If they do:

1. Their sins will be **forgiven**
2. They'll get the gift of the **Holy Spirit**

Verse 39 means that this promise is for **us** too—even though we live 2000 years after Peter! Peter says our sins can be forgiven because of **Jesus**. Turn to **God's Rescue Plan** on the next page to find out more.

Joe can pretend the broken window is nothing to do with him—or he can own up and **do something about it**.

Like Joe, the people who heard Peter's speech can pretend it's nothing to do with them—or own up and **do something about it**. What will they do…?

### READ
Acts 2v37-40

**THINK SPOT**
- Have you been forgiven by Jesus?
- Do you want to be?
(Read **God's Rescue Plan** again if you're not sure.)

**PRAY**
To repent doesn't just mean saying sorry. It means asking God to help you to **change**, and to do what He says. Do you want God to help you to change? If so, pray now.

# GOD'S RESCUE PLAN

**Why** did God rescue us—and **who** is the Rescuer? John 3v16 explains it.

## God loved the world so much...

This is the reason for the Rescue Plan. God's **everlasting love** for you and me. He wants us to know Him and to be His friends. But there's a problem. SIN gets in the way.

### What is Sin?

We all like to be in charge of our own lives. We do what **we** want instead of what **God** wants. This is called Sin.

Sin gets in the way between us and God. It stops us from knowing Him and stops us from being His friends. The final result of sin is death. You can see why we need to be rescued!

## ...that He gave His only Son...

God sent Jesus to be our Rescuer—to save us from the problem of sin.

### How did Jesus rescue us?

At the first Easter, when Jesus was about 33 years old, He was crucified. He was nailed to a cross and left to die.

As He died, all the sins of the world (all the wrongs people do) were put onto Jesus. He took all of our sin onto Himself, taking the punishment we deserve. He died in our place, as our Rescuer, so that we can be forgiven.

*Did you know?*

Jesus died on the cross as our Rescuer—but He didn't stay dead! After three days God brought Him back to life! Jesus is still alive today, ruling as our King.

## ...so that everyone who believes in Him may not die but have eternal life. (John 3v16)

When Jesus died He dealt with the problem of sin. That means that there is nothing to separate us from God any more. That's great news for you and me!

We can know God today as our Friend and King—and one day live in heaven with Him for ever.

Have YOU been rescued by Jesus? Turn to the next page to find out more...

# AM I A CHRISTIAN?

**Not sure if you're a Christian? Then check it out below...**

Christians are people who have been rescued by Jesus and follow Him as their King.

> **You can't become a Christian by trying to be good.**

That's great news, since you can't be totally good all the time!

It's about accepting what Jesus did on the cross to rescue you. To do that, you will need to **ABCD**.

**A** **Admit** your sin—that you do, say and think wrong things. Tell God you are sorry. Ask Him to forgive you, and to help you to change. There will be some wrong things you have to stop doing.

**B** **Believe** that Jesus died for you, to take the punishment for your sin; that He came back to life, and that He is still alive today.

**C** **Consider** the cost of living like God's friend from now on, with Him in charge. It won't be easy. Ask God to help you do this.

**D** **Do** something about it! In the past you've gone your own way rather than God's way. Will you hand control of your life over to Him from now on? If you're ready to ABCD, then talk to God now. The prayer will help you.

**A prayer**

Dear God,
I have done and said and thought things that are wrong. I am really sorry. Please forgive me. Thank you for sending Jesus to die for me. From now on, please help me to live as one of Your friends, with You in charge.     Amen

> **Do you remember Jesus' promise?**—"everyone who believes in Him shall not die but have eternal life."
> John 3v16

> **Jesus welcomes everyone who comes to Him. If you have put your trust in Him, He has rescued you from your sins and will help you to live for Him. That's great news!**

# DAY 8 GROWING ALL THE TIME

## READ
### Acts 2v41-47

How many people believed Peter's message? (v41)

**3?    30?    300?    3000?**

The new believers were all baptised. It must have taken **ages**!

### Did You Know?

Getting baptised means being washed in water to show that you follow Jesus.
Being **baptised** is like being washed on the **outside**.
Being **forgiven** is like being washed on the **inside**.
Baptism is an **outside** sign of an **inside** change.

Cross out every **X** & **Z** to find out what the new believers were like.

**SXHXAZRXIZNZG** with each other

**XGZIXVXIZNZG** to those in need

**MZEZEXTZIXNXG** together **DZAXIZLXY**

**PZRZAXIZSZIXNZG** God together

The believers were like this because the Holy Spirit was changing them on the inside.

*Now fit the five words into the puzzle below.*

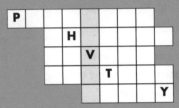

What word do the shaded boxes spell?    **S**

Every day the Lord added to their group those who were being **S_____** (v47)

This means more and more people with the nickname **Christians** — because they had become followers of **Jesus Christ**.

## PRAY

Look again at the list of words in the puzzle.
Do you want to live like this?
Talk to God about your answer.

# DAY 9 THE THREE O'CLOCK MIRACLE

## READ
### Acts 3v1-10

Spot the mistakes in the story below. There are **ten** to find.
Circle each one.

> One day Peter and Paul were going to the cinema. It was five o'clock in the afternoon. They saw a lame camel, standing by the Ugly Gate. He asked them for jam tarts. Peter said, "Wink at us! I have loads of money, but I'll give you something better. In the name of Jesus Christ of Norway, get up and ski."

*Read verse 6 again.*
*Copy the last part of the verse into the box.*

**In the name of**

It wasn't Peter who made this man well.
It was **Jesus!**

What was the man doing as he went into the Temple? (v8)

w_____ ing
j_____ ing
p_____ ing God

THINK SPOT

- Why could the man **walk**?
- Why do you think he was **jumping**?
- Why was he **praising** God?

He was **so excited**. He could walk again! He easily could have forgotten to thank God. **But he didn't!**

## PRAY

It's easy to forget to thank God for the great things He has given us. Think of some things to thank and praise God for. Then do it!

# DAY 10 CHATTERBOX TIME

**Wow!** A man who has been lame all his life is suddenly cured! *Imagine the excitement...*

Can you do a cartwheel?

Tell us what happened!

How do you feel?

Can Peter cure my sore toe?

What's your Mum think about it?

Then the crowds turn to Peter. He seems to be the guy who did it all. What will he say?

## READ
### Acts 3v11-16

Peter doesn't talk about **himself** —and says very little about the **miracle**. **Who** does he talk about instead?(v16)

J_____

The Holy Spirit is helping Peter to be a **chatterbox** about Jesus. Just as Jesus had promised.

**Fill in the gaps in verse 15.**

*Use these words.* → life / killed / dead / God

You _____ the one who gives _____, but _____ raised him from the _____.(v15)

It sounds a bit like Peter's last speech doesn't it?
- **not** very popular stuff!
- **not** what the people were expecting
- but it's what they **needed** to hear (as we'll see on Day 12).

*If you want to sneak a peak at how people react, check out Acts 4v4.*

## THINK + PRAY

Notice how Peter takes every opportunity to be a chatterbox for Jesus. Do **you**? Who can you tell about Jesus this week? Write their name here.

_____

Ask God to help you.

# DAY 11 SIGNPOSTS

**John's** book about Jesus (John's Gospel) tells us something mega-important about miracles...

> These miracles have been written down so that you may believe that Jesus is the Christ, the Son of God, and that by believing you may have life in His name.
>
> John 20v31

*Underline* the words that tell us **who Jesus is.** (Circle) the words that say **what we should do.**

Jesus' miracles are like **SIGNPOSTS**, pointing to **Jesus**. They show us **WHO Jesus is** and **WHAT we should do.**

---

Peter's miracle was like a signpost too. It pointed to **Jesus**.

## READ
### Acts 3v16

*Fill in the gaps.*
*They all say the same name!*

> Peter made it clear to the crowd that J_____ did this.

> Dead men don't do miracles. But J_____ didn't stay dead! He came back to life!

> Even though people couldn't see J_____ any more — He really was alive. This miracle was a signpost pointing straight at J_____

---

This page is all about **JESUS**. *Count up how many times the name **Jesus** is on the page.*

**WOW!** **Jesus is still alive today. We can't see Him or touch Him— but we can know that He is with us. Jesus sends us His Spirit to live inside us and help us to follow Him.**

## THINK + PRAY

**What day is it today?**

_____

**Dear Jesus, thank you that You are still alive today. Please help me to follow you always.**
**Amen**

# DAY 12 PROMISED LONG AGO

The crowd Peter was speaking to were Jewish—so they knew all about these people from the Old Testament part of the Bible...

### MOSES
God promised that He would send a **PROPHET** (God's messenger) like Moses. The people must listen to this new prophet.

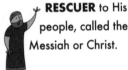

### THE PROPHETS
The Old Testament prophets spoke of a time when God would send a **RESCUER** to His people, called the Messiah or Christ.

### ABRAHAM
God promised that one of Abraham's family would be God's way of **BLESSING** the whole world.

Peter showed that **Jesus** came as the answer to **all three promises...**

**READ**
Acts 3v22-26

Peter said that Jesus was...
*(Fill in the missing letters: e, i + o)*

- The **pr_ph_t** like Moses
- The **r_scu_r** the prophets spoke about
- The **bl_ss_ng** who came from Abraham's family

God kept His promises. **Stick a Promise sticker here**

PROMISE

So what did Peter tell the people to do?

**READ**
Acts 3v19

It's the same message as before—to **turn away** from sin and **turn towards** God—but it's about to get Peter into BIG trouble, as we'll see tomorrow...

**PRAY**

God promised that Jesus would come—and He did! He came to rescue His people and bless the whole world—just as God had said. Thank God that we can trust Him to **always** do what He says.

# DAY 13 B—I—G TROUBLE

A lame man has been **cured**, and Peter has been teaching the **great news** about Jesus. Follow the maze to see what happens next to Peter and John—and to the group of believers.

Peter & John

5000+

The believers

**What did you find?** *Copy the pictures here.*

Peter & John ☐   The believers ☐

Peter and John spent the night in **prison**, because they told the **truth** about Jesus. Next morning they're dragged in front of the Jewish Council. These were the men **who had Jesus killed!**

What will Peter say...?

### READ
Acts 4v7-12

**Wow!** Even after a night in prison, Peter is still being a chatterbox!
Who helped him? (v8) **The H_____ S_____**

Who does Peter say is the ONLY way to be saved? (v12) ➡ 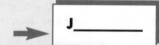 **J_____**

And look what happened to the believers.
**Read v4**. Now there's more than 5000 of them! And that's just the **men**! There would have been lots of women and children too.

**Think Spot**

Do your friends laugh at you for following Jesus? Or say that church is b-o-r-i-n-g? The Holy Spirit will help you to stand up for Jesus—just as He helped Peter.

**PRAY**  **Ask God to help you to stand up for Jesus—even if that means being laughed at sometimes.**

# DAY 14 — STOP TALKING!

Acts 4v13-22

## The story so far...

*Draw in the faces—here are a few ideas.*

A man had been lame for over 40 years. ◯ Now he was cured. ◯ The crowds were amazed! ◯ Peter told them they had turned their backs on God ◯ but that Jesus had come to save them. ◯ Lots of people became believers. ◯ The Jewish leaders were angry, ◯ and threw Peter and John into prison. ◯ But the Holy Spirit helped them to be brave ◯ and to keep telling people about Jesus.

Peter knew that God had to come **first**—no matter what happened. The Jewish council were very powerful—but God was **more powerful**.

## READ
### Acts 4v13

The Jewish council realised why Peter and John were so **bold**. Because they had been with **J_____**

 The council decided to tell Peter and John to **stop** being chatterboxes!

## READ
### Acts 4v18-22

Peter and John have been told **not** to talk about Jesus.
Did Peter agree? (v20) ✔ ✗

The council warned them **again** not to talk about Jesus—and let them go.

## THINK + PRAY

Does God come first in **your** life? What about when your friends want you to tell lies for them? Or you can't be bothered to go to church or read your Bible? Think about the times when you find it hard to put God first. Ask God to help you—just like He helped Peter and John.

# DAY 15 **BE BOLD!**

Peter and John have been set free from prison—but told **not** to talk about Jesus again! So what did they do? They asked God to help them **be bold**—and to keep talking about Jesus!

**READ**
**Acts 4v23-30**

The believers reminded themselves of what **God is like**. Crack the code to see what they remembered.

God is ♦ ▼ ⊛ ● _ _ _ _ (v24)

God ❖ ◗ ■ ○ _ _ _ _ everything (v24)

God is in ▢ ▲ ◗ ✿ ● ○ _ _ _ _ _ _ (v28)

**Wow!** You can see why they are so sure that God can help them!

## BOLD CODE

A = ◗
C = ▢
D = ■
E = ○
G = ●
H = ▲
I = ▼
K = ♦
M = ❖
N = ⊛
R = ✿
S = ✳
W = ✴

So how did God answer their prayer?

**READ**
**Acts 4v31**

The room **shook**! They were filled with the **Holy Spirit**. And spoke about Jesus **BOLDLY**!

**Why did this happen?**

God ◗ ⊛ ✳ ✴ ○ ✿ ✳

God _ _ _ _ _ _ _ prayer

**THINK + PRAY**

I have a sign above my door that says "**God is able**". When I pray, it reminds me that God is able to answer all my prayers. What difference does it make to you that God is your **King**, who made **everything** and is **in charge** of our world? Thank God that He is able to answer all your prayers.

# INTRODUCING GENESIS

Do you like history?  **Yippee!**  **Yeurch!**

**HISTORY** is **HIS STORY**

It is **God's** Story

—and we're starting right at the very beginning with the book of **Genesis**.

**GENESIS** is a Greek word.
Crack the Creation Code
to find out what it means.

 = **B**   = **G**   = **N**

 = **E**   = **I**   = **S**

— — — — — — — — — —

**Genesis is a book of beginnings.**

- The beginning of the **universe**.
- The beginning of the **human race**.
- The beginning of God's special family, **the Israelites**.

**In Genesis, we see what God is like.**

⭐ We see God as the **Star-Maker** and **Promise-Giver**. (So be ready to stick in some Promise stickers.)

⭐ We see that God is **King** of the world that He made.

⭐ Sadly, we also see that people don't want Him to be their King.

**Let's start at the very beginning...**

## DAY 16
CONTINUED

# IN THE BEGINNING...

**Finish each picture.**

When you draw a picture you need
- something to draw with
- and paper to put it on.

But God is **so powerful** that He created the universe out of absolutely nothing!

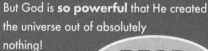

### READ
**Genesis 1v1-5**

---

Before anything else existed, **God** was already there.
He created EVERYTHING—just by saying it must be made!

> **Wow**!
> God needed no help or tools or even cosmic dust to make it from! God just spoke—and the universe was made!

What was the first thing that God said? (v3)
*Unjumble the words*

**be    there    light    Let**

___  ___  ___  ___

**WOW!**  God spoke. Just a word. That was enough for light to burst into the world!

---

Imagine if there was **no light**—and everything was always dark. You couldn't play football, watch TV or go roller blading. Even eating sausages would be tricky!

**What else couldn't you do?**

1 _____

2 _____

3 _____

You can see why light is so **good**! (v4)

**PRAY**  Thank God for creating our world, and for the light to see and enjoy it.

# HE ALSO MADE THE STARS

Genesis 1v6-25

## READ
### Genesis 1v6-25

*Fill in
the gaps*

 birds    animals    plants

stars    sky    night

**Day 1**
(v3-5)

Day &
n_____

**Day 2**
(v6-8)

S_____ &
water

**Day 3**
(v9-13)

Sea, land &
p_____

**Day 4**
(v14-19)

Sun, moon
& s_____

**Day 5**
(v20-23)

Fish &
b_____

**Day 6**
(v24-31)

A_____
& people

*Did You Know?*
There are over 10,000,000,000,000,000,000,000 stars! And God has named each one! (Psalm 147v4)

How many kinds of **plant** did God make? (v11)
one?          a few?          loads?
Some that look great, or smell nice, or taste scrummy,
or give us medicines or are good to climb or...

How many kinds of **animal** did God make? (v24)
one?          a few?          loads?
Which is your favourite? _____

> Did you spot the words that keep popping up? (*In v4, 10, 12, 18, 21, 25.*)
> ### God saw that it was good.
> (Some Bibles say "God was pleased with what he saw" instead.)

Whichever words your Bible uses, they mean that what God
made is **GREAT**—and just how **God planned it**. None of it happened
by accident!

**THINK
+
PRAY**

When you pray, you're talking to the **Person** who
created everything—including **you**! Think of some of your
favourite things in our world. Stars? Spiders? Snow?
Strawberries? Seahorses? Now thank God for making
them.

# DAY 18 SPOT THE DIFFERENCE!

| A duck | You |
|---|---|
|  | Draw yourself or sign your name |

What's the difference between you and a duck? (!)

Genesis says you are **very different** from a duck!

## READ
### Genesis 1v26-31

Human beings are made in **God's likeness** (v26). That means made like God Himself!

 **WOW!**

- **We** are like God.
- Animals and birds (and ducks!) are **not** like God.

---

In what way are people made like God? (*Cross out the x's*)

**"They will rxuxlxe over the fxixsxh, birds and axnxixmxaxlxs."** (v26)

God has put us **in charge** of His world, to look after it and enjoy it.

**THINK SPOT**

God created a good world for us to live in. What can **you** do to look after God's world?

---

What did God do when He had finished creating the world? (v2)

## READ
### Genesis 2v1-3

God didn't stop because He was tired! He stopped because He had **finished** His work, and it was exactly how He planned it. Everything was perfect.

So what's God doing now?

God finished creating the world, but He carried on caring for it and helping His people.

**PRAY**

Think again about your answer to the **Think Spot**. Ask God to help you.

# DAY 19 WHOSE JOB IS IT ANYWAY?

## READ
### Genesis 2v4-9

*Fill in the missing vowels:* ☆=a;
★=e; ✪=i; ✳=o; ☆=u

- The world is G✳d's place.
  He cr★☆t★d it. (v4)

- God created the first m☆n out of d☆st!
  God gave him l✪f★. (v7)

- God made a p★rf★ct g☆rd★n for
  the man to live in. (v8)

## READ
### Genesis 2v15-17

- Man was put in the garden to w✳rk and
  t☆k★ c☆r★ of it. (v15)

- God is K✪NG. It is **His job** to decide what
  is g✳✳d and b☆d. (v17)

There's one tree that the man **must not** eat from.
Which tree is it? (v17)

**The tr__ __ of the knowledge of g __ __ d and b __ d.**

> If the man eats from this tree, he will want to decide for himself
> what's good and what's bad. But that's **God's job!**

We can put this all together in a picture. *Fill in the gaps*

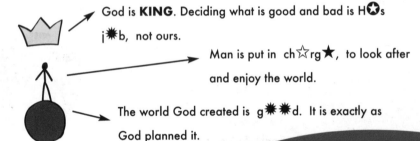

God is **KING**. Deciding what is good and bad is H✪s
j✳b, not ours.

Man is put in ch☆rg★, to look after
and enjoy the world.

The world God created is g✳✳d. It is exactly as
God planned it.

### THINK + PRAY

God gave the man a **choice**. He could obey
God—or he could eat from the tree. We have the **same
choice**. We can obey God and live for Him, or turn our backs
on God and live our own way. Do **you** want to obey God and
live for Him? If so, ask Him to help you.

# DAY 20 SHE'S THE ONE

The first man—**Adam**—is living in a perfect garden, in a perfect world. But something is missing...

**READ**
Genesis 2v18-20

**What did God say?**
(v18)

> It is n _ _ g _ _ _ _ for the man to be a _ _ _ _ _

So Adam met all the birds and animals. He chose names for them all. *Can you match these unusual animals to their names?*

A

B

C

D

E

F

Aadvark
Bandicoot
Gnu
Gopher
Llama
Sloth

God had created an **amazing** bunch of animals—but none of them could be Adam's companion, because people are **completely different** from animals. *Look again at Day 18 if you're not sure why.*

So, how did God solve the problem?

**READ**
Genesis 2v21-25

> **God made a w _ _ _ _ _ out of Adam's r _ _** (v22)

Sounds painful! But Adam felt no pain because God put him into a deep sleep.

The woman was just what Adam wanted! She was **like** him—but **different**. The perfect companion.

*She's the one!*

*Did You Know?*

Adam's wife was very special to him, because she came from his own body. (v23) God says all marriages are special—**two** people come together and form **one** partnership.

**PRAY**

Thank God for creating both men and women. Thank Him too for His great gift of marriage.

# DAY 21 SNAKES AND LADDERS

Do you remember what we discovered on Day 19?

God is **KING**. Deciding what is g __ __ d and b __ d is **His job**, not ours.

**BUT** there's someone in the garden who wants to spoil everything...

## READ
**Genesis 3v1-7**

Follow the snake down the middle of the page. *Use these words to fill in the gaps.*

Adam
ate
Eve
lies
more

The snake told
I _____ about
God. (v1,4,5)

**E** _____ listened to the snake's lies. (v1,6)

Eve wanted
**m** _____ than
God had given
her. (v6)

Eve took the fruit and
**a** _____ it. (v6)

She gave some fruit to
**A** _____ (v6)

Adam and Eve had **broken God's rule**. They wanted to decide for themselves what was good and bad.

We don't want **you** to be King!

They chose to do what **they** wanted instead of what **God** wanted. This is called **SIN**.

## PRAY

The snake was the devil in disguise. The devil always wants us to disobey God. Ask God to help you **not to listen** to the devil's tempting ideas.

# DAY 22 SIN SNAPSHOTS

Adam and Eve have disobeyed God. They have **sinned**. These snapshots show what happened next. *Copy each picture into the right photo frame.*

**1**
Adam & Eve hide from God among the <u>trees</u>.

**2**
Adam <u>blames</u> Eve. Eve <u>blames</u> the snake.

**3**
The <u>snake</u> is cursed by God, and will be hated by people.

**4**
God says <u>Eve</u> will now have great pain when she gives birth to children.

**5**
God says Adam will have to <u>work</u> very hard to grow enough food to eat.

**6**
They are banned from the garden. A flaming <u>sword</u> keeps them away from the tree of life.

## READ
### Genesis 3v8-15

*If you have time, read the rest of the story in verses 16-24.*

The snake, the woman and the man have all been punished by God. Adam and Eve have been sent out of the garden, away from the tree of life. They won't live with God for ever (as they were meant to). Instead, they will **die**. This is the result of **SIN**.

But in the middle of all this **punishment**, there's a great **promise** too...

**Read verse 15 again.**
"Her offspring will crush your head."

 THINK SPOT
It sounds odd doesn't it? But God is promising that one of Eve's family (her offspring) will beat the devil (the snake). This promise is all about **Jesus**—who came as our Rescuer to beat the problem of sin for ever.

**Stick a Promise sticker here**

 PROMISE

PRAY
Sin separates us from God. But Jesus came to solve the problem of sin, so that we can be forgiven. Thank God for keeping His promise to send Jesus as our Rescuer.

# DAY 23 THE BEST WAY TO LIVE

> We don't want **you** to be King!

It's tempting to think that being in charge of our own lives must be better than being told what to do. **But God knows the BEST way for us to live.**

This horrible story shows us what happens when people live **without** God's rule.

**1** Adam & Eve had two sons. Cain was a farmer. Abel was a shepherd.

**2** Cain and Abel both gave an offering (a gift) to God. Cain gave God some of his crops.

**3** Abel gave God the best of his flock. God was pleased with Abel's gift— but not with Cain's.

**4** Cain was so angry that he took his brother Abel out to a field, and **killed** him.

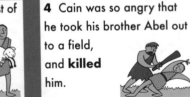

**Look how sin spreads**:

- Cain is **a**_____ (v6) —even when God says he shouldn't be.
- As a result, Cain commits the first **m**_____ (v8).
- And then he **l**_____ to God about it...

> Fit these words in the gaps:
> *lies    angry    murder*

## READ
### Genesis 4v8-12

> When God asked where Abel was, what did Cain say? (v9)
> **I d**_____  **k**_____

Cain lied, but **God knew** what he had done, and punished him for his sin. Cain wasn't able to grow crops any more. He became a wanderer, with no home. Verse 16 says that Cain was separated from God as a result.

> Look at what sin does. It **spreads** (*getting worse and worse, as we will see tomorrow*). And it **separates** us from God.

**THINK + PRAY**

Say **sorry** to God for the last time that you disobeyed Him. **Thank** God that He's given us loads of help in the Bible to show us the best way to live.

# DAY 24 BUILD A LIFEBOAT

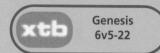

xtb — Genesis 6v5-22

Look at how much has changed between chapter one and chapter six of Genesis:

**CHAPTER ONE**
God saw all that He had **made**, and it was very **good**.

Genesis 1v31

**CHAPTER SIX**
The Lord was **sorry** that He had made **man** ... and His heart was filled with **pain**.

Genesis 6v6

*Find the underlined words in the puzzle. Some are backwards.*

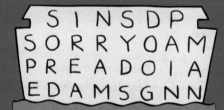

```
S I N S D P
S O R R Y O A M
P R E A D O I A
E D A M S G N N
```

The rest of the letters spell out what the problem was. Copy them here. **S _ _ S _ _ _ _ _ _ _**

God was so sorry that He had made man, that He decided to flood the earth clean. But there was one man who did obey God...

## READ
### Genesis 6v8-22

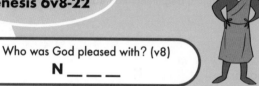

Who was God pleased with? (v8)
**N _ _ _**

God told Noah what He planned to do—that He would flood the earth. But God **promised** that Noah and his family would be kept safe.

**Stick a Promise sticker here** ➡ PROMISE

THINK SPOT

Imagine being told to build a h-u-g-e boat—miles away from the sea! Would you do it? What would your friends say?

**PRAY**
Read verse 22 again. Do you want to obey God as completely as Noah did? Then ask God to help you.

# DAY 25 INTO THE ARK

Think of an animal beginning with each of these letters:

N

O

A advark

H

S

A

R

K

The ark had to carry **loads more animals** than these! It was like a giant lifeboat to keep Noah's family and all the animals and birds safe.

### READ
### Genesis 7v1-10

How many pairs of clean animals? (v2) ☐

How many pairs of unclean animals? ☐

*Did you know?*

The **clean** animals (like sheep) weren't better at washing than the others! They were the ones that could be offered to God as a gift.



**xtb** Genesis 7v1-10

Noah had to do some **hard things** for God
- build a huge boat
- fill the boat with food for the animals and birds
- believe the flood would happen even though the sun was shining!

But God didn't tell Noah to do anything **impossible**. God knew that Noah couldn't catch all those animals on his own—so God made the animals **come** to Noah! (v9)

**Noah obeyed God.**

**THINK + PRAY**

Read verse 5 again.
Noah obeyed God by doing the things he **could** do—and trusted God to look after the rest. God doesn't expect **you** to do impossible stuff either! Ask God to help you to obey what He says, and to trust Him to look after the things that seem impossible.

**The animals obeyed God.**

**The flood obeyed God.**

**1** The Bible fits together like a GIANT JIGSAW.

All the way through we find **the same two things:**
1 Sin must be punished.
2 God provides a way to be rescued.

**2** SIN MUST BE PUNISHED
God's perfect world had been made dirty by sin. It needed to be washed clean.

**READ**
Genesis 7v17-24

How long did the flood waters keep coming? (v17)
_____ **days**

**3** GOD PROVIDES A RESCUE
God provided a way to be rescued from the flood. Who was rescued? (v23)

N_____ and
_____

**4** Why were Noah and his family rescued?

• They were perfect ✔✘

• They were good swimmers ✔✘

• They trusted God to rescue them ✔✘

**5** SIN MUST BE PUNISHED
Everyone sins. We **all** disobey God.

GOD PROVIDES A RESCUE
**Who** does the Bible say is the greatest Rescuer of all?
J_____

*Do you know why? Check Matthew 1v21 for the answer.*

**6** **PRAY** All sin has to be punished— including yours and mine. Thank God for sending Jesus to rescue us.

# DAY 27 GOD REMEMBERS NOAH

How do you remember things? My friend writes on the back of her hand. My dad puts a knot in his tie— and then forgets why!

What do **you** do?

Genesis 8v1 says, "God **remembered** Noah." God doesn't forget things! When God "remembered" Noah, it means He **acted** on His promise to Noah. God always keeps His promises.

## READ
### Genesis 8v6-14

How did Noah check if the water had gone down?

How long did Noah and his family live on the ark?
- a) 40 days and nights
- b) about 4 months
- c) over a year

Check your answer at the bottom of the page.

**THINK SPOT**

Imagine spending a year on a boat with all those animals. Think about the **noise**! And the **smell**! Why do you think Noah kept trusting God all that time? Do you think he found it easy?

God had promised to keep Noah and his family safe. God **kept** His promise.

**THINK + PRAY**

**Stick a Promise sticker here.** →

Ask God to help you to trust Him patiently, just as Noah did.

# DAY 28 OUT OF THE ARK

After a year in a noisy, smelly boat, at last it's time to step back onto dry land. How do you think Noah felt? *Circle your answers & add more of your own.*

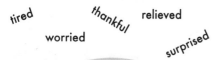

tired

thankful   relieved

worried

surprised

## READ
### Genesis 8v15-20

How did Noah know it was time to leave the ark? (v15-16)

Noah wanted to thank God for saving him and his family. Do you remember how many pairs of **clean** animals and birds Noah took on the ark? *(See Day 25 to check.)*
Noah took some of these and used them as an offering to thank God.

God was pleased with Noah's offering and thankfulness. He decided never to destroy the earth like this again.

## READ
### Genesis 8v21-22

God promised that as long as the earth exists there will be **cold**, **heat**, **summer**, **winter**, **day** and **night**.

**Has God kept His promise?** _____

**Fill in the red words from verse 22.**

I'm writing this on New Year's Day, looking out at the **snow**! For me it's **cold**, **winter** and **day**. What's **your** weather like right now?

## PRAY

Look again at the list in verse 22. Thank God that these things remind you that God is keeping His promise to take care of our world.

# RAINBOW PROMISES

Genesis 9v1-17

Do you know the colours of the rainbow?

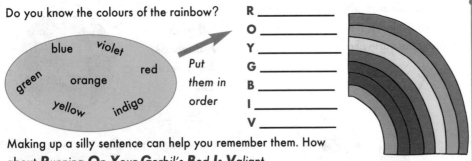

blue  violet
green  orange  red
yellow  indigo

*Put them in order*

R _____
O _____
Y _____
G _____
B _____
I _____
V _____

Making up a silly sentence can help you remember them. How about *Running On Your Gerbil's Bed Is Valiant* ...or try one of your own.

The flood is over at last. In verses 1-7 God tells Noah and his family how they are to live from now on. Then God makes them an amazing promise (called a covenant).

## READ
### Genesis 9v7-17

What does God promise Noah? (v11) ➡️

Never to...

What was the sign that God would keep His promise? (v13) ➡️

### RAINBOW CHALLENGE
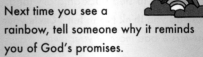
Next time you see a rainbow, tell someone why it reminds you of God's promises.

God knew that His rules would keep being broken. But He gave people the whole of the earth to live in and enjoy. And He promised never to send another flood. What does that tell you about what God is like?

### PRAY

"The Lord is good to everyone and has compassion on all He made." *Psalm 145v9* Thank God that He is like this.

# DAY 30 A PERFECT MAN?

Noah and his family were **not** perfect! At the end of Genesis 9, Noah plants the first vineyard, turns the grapes into wine—and gets drunk! (*There is only* **one** *perfect man. We start reading about Him tomorrow.*)

Noah wasn't perfect—but there's still loads to learn from his life. Read what the New Testament part of the Bible says about him...

**READ**
Hebrews 11v7

**Noah had** _ _ _ _ _ **in God.**

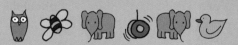

**Noah** _ _ _ _ _ _ **God.**

**THINK SPOT**

Think about all you've learnt about God in the book of Genesis. (*Check Days 23 and 27 to help you.*) Does this help you to trust and obey God as Noah did? Why?

**PRAY**

Dear God,

Thank you that You always keep Your promises. Please help me to **trust** You.

Thank you that You know the best way for me to live. Please help me to **obey** You.

Amen

# MATTHEW MATTERS

**Welcome to Matthew's book about Jesus, with some special bits to look out for as you read it.**

## Bits from other books

Matthew squeezed in loads of chunks from the Old Testament. **Why?** Because the Old T is full of promises about a new king.

Matthew shows us that **JESUS** is this promised King.

## PROMISES

Here are **three promises** from the Old Testament to look out for.

Be ready to stick in a Promise sticker each time you find one.

### To Abraham
God promised that one of Abraham's family would be God's way of **blessing** the whole world.

### To David
God promised that one of David's family would be a **King** who would rule for ever and ever.

### To God's people
God promised that He would send a **rescuer**, called the Messiah or Christ.

## Waiting, waiting...

Do you find it hard to wait for things?

It had been 2000 years since Abraham...

...1000 years since David...

...600 years since the promise to send a rescuer.

Had God changed His mind? Maybe He'd forgotten!

No way! God's not like that. Read on to see what Matthew tells us about the new King...

Some families are huge. Some tiny.
What's yours like?
Write their names in some (or all!) of the boxes on the family tree.

## READ
### Matthew 1v1

Matthew starts his book with a family tree.

**Whose family is it?** J_____

Verses 2-16 give a l-o-n-g list of names.

Seems a bit boring? Actually, it's dynamite!

**Do you remember the three Old Testament promises?**
*Check them out on the previous page.* **Now find some names in Jesus' family tree:**

A_____ (See verse 2)   J O_____ (See verse 16)

D_____ (See verse 6)   M____ (See verse 16)

**Find all these names in the wordsearch.** *(Some are written backwards!)*

| | | | | | | | | | | |
|---|---|---|---|---|---|---|---|---|---|---|
| J | E | A | B | R | A | H | A | M | S | Y |
| U | S | W | H | O | I | S | C | A | L | R |
| L | E | D | I | V | A | D | D | C | H | A |
| J | O | S | E | P | H | R | I | S | T | M |

Copy the left over letters here.

_ _ _ _ _  _ _ _
_ _ _ _ _ _  _ _ _ _ _ _

*(Check with verse 16)*

Christ (or Messiah) means "God's chosen King".
**Stick a Promise sticker** here to remind you that
God kept His promise to send Jesus as King. →

## PRAY
God kept His promise to send King Jesus. Thank God for always keeping His promises.

# DAY 32 A KING IS BORN

When is your birthday?

How long do you have to wait?
- **Nearly a year?**
- **Months & months?**
- **A few weeks?**
- **A few days?** (*I bet you're excited!*)

God's people had been waiting a **very long time** for Him to send the new King. Now at last the time had come.

## READ
### Matthew 1v18-21

Crack the star code to see what the name **Jesus** means.

✻=A ✺=D ✲=E ★=G
✹=H ☆=I ☆=O ✪=S
✸=T ✳=U ★=V ☆=W

It tells us **who** Jesus is — He is **G** _ _

It tells us **what** Jesus does — He **S** _ _ _ _ _

## READ
### Matthew 1v22-23

Did you spot the promise to send Jesus?
**Stick a Promise sticker here.** ➡️

Jesus is given another great name here.
What does **Immanuel** mean?

☆ ☆ ✻   ☆ ☆ ✺ ✸   ✸ ✪

_ _ _   _ _ _ _   _ _

## PRAY
These brilliant names tell us loads about Jesus. Choose **one** to give thanks to God for.

# WISE MEN WORSHIP JESUS

 Matthew 2v1-11

Copy every **second** letter to find two good kings, both born in Bethlehem.

K **D** I **A** N V G I F D O **J** R E E S V U E S R

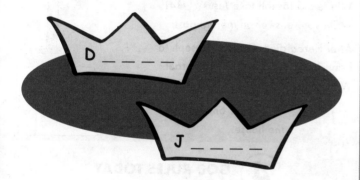

D _ _ _ _ _

J _ _ _ _ _

The other letters remind us of God's promise to King David.

**"Someone from your family will be**

k _ _ _ f _ _ e _ _ _ ."

**READ**
**Matthew 2v1-2**

Looking for the new king, the wise men went to the palace in Jerusalem. They did find a king there—**evil** King Herod!

Herod didn't want anyone else to be king, so he made secret plans to murder Jesus. **More about that tomorrow.**

**READ**
**Matthew 2v9-11**

The wise men reached Jesus at last. He's just a little toddler. But what do these important visitors do? (v11). *Write or draw your answer.*

**SPOT THE DIFFERENCE!**
• the wise men **worship** Jesus
• king Herod only **pretends**

**THINK + PRAY**

Do you really worship Jesus? Or are you just pretending? What can **you** do to worship Jesus?

# DAY 34 ESCAPE TO EGYPT

Matthew 2v12-23

## 1 THE STORY SO FAR

**SECRET?**
Herod's secret plan was to murder the new king.

**READ**
Matthew 2v12

**NO SECRET!**
God warned the wise men not to go back to **H** _____

God made sure that the wise men didn't tell Herod where Jesus was. **God was in control.**

## 2 ESCAPE!

**READ**
Matthew 2v13-14

Where did Joseph take Jesus? (v14)
*Write your answer on the signpost.*

After Herod died, God told Joseph to bring Jesus and Mary back to Israel. Which town did they live in? (v23)

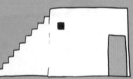

*Write your answer in the house.*

**GOD IS IN CONTROL**

## 3 GOD ALWAYS KNEW

**READ**
Matthew 2v16-18

Herod's plans were horrible. But God told the writers of the Old T _____ all about them 100s of years before they happened!

Herod wanted to spoil God's promise of a new King, but he couldn't! Who was in control? **G** _____

## 4 GOD RULES TODAY

God is always in control. This means:

★ at home     ★ at school

★ with friends     ★ when bad things happen

**PRAY** How does this make you feel? Talk to God about it.

# LOCUSTS FOR LUNCH

## READ
## Matthew 3v1-6

**Circle the mistakes in this picture**

Everything's Cool!

John the Baptist

Check verses 2 & 4, then draw the correct version here.

Did you spot the Old Testament chunk? (in verse 3.) God promised to send a messenger to His people, to tell them "Get ready for the King".

God kept His promise by sending John the Baptist as His messenger. **Stick a Promise sticker here.**

PROMISE

John didn't say "Everything's cool" because it wasn't! The people weren't ready for their King. They hadn't been living the way God wanted them to.

What did John tell them to do? (v2)

John baptised people in the river Jordan. It showed that they wanted to be washed clean from all their wrongs (their sins), ready to welcome King Jesus.

**THINK + PRAY**

Is anything stopping **you** from welcoming Jesus as your King? Say sorry and ask Him to help you to change.

# DAY 36 ROTTEN APPLES?

xtb Matthew 3v7-12

**Follow the lines to match the pairs.**

## Pictures 1 + B

John's job was to help people get ready for the new King. The **religious leaders** should have done the same, but didn't. So John called them **snakes**!

## Pictures A + 3

John is telling people to stop living for themselves (repent from sin) and turn to King Jesus. If they do this their lives will change. They will be like **good trees** producing **good fruit**.

## Pictures C + 2

But if they don't repent, they will be like **bad trees** which end up being **destroyed**. People who don't live for God will be cut off from Him for ever.

## READ
### Matthew 3v7-10

John talks about snakes, good fruit and rotten fruit. Spot which verse matches each pair from the puzzle.

Verse 7 matches _____
Verse 8 matches _____
Verse 10 matches _____

## THINK + PRAY

To repent doesn't just mean saying sorry. It means asking God to help you to **change**, and to do what He says. Are you ready to repent? If so, pray now.

# THE KING IS BAPTISED

## READ
### Matthew 3v13-17

The picture shows John baptising Jesus. At the top, draw in what happened next (verses 16 & 17).

The people who came to John admitted that they were sinful and needed to be forgiven. John baptised **sinners** who **repented**. But what surprising thing did Jesus want John to do? (v13)

Jesus was **perfect**. He never sinned, and had no need to repent. As we'll see tomorrow, Jesus always obeyed God. That's why Jesus was baptised. Not to repent, but to obey God (v15).

What did God say about Jesus? (v17)

1. JESUS IS GOD'S S_____

2. GOD L_____ JESUS

3. GOD IS P_____

WITH JESUS

 **xtb** Matthew 3v13-17

God loved Jesus. But He still sent His greatly loved Son to save us by dying in our place, so that our sins can be forgiven. That shows how much God loves us!

## THINK+ PRAY

What does the name Jesus mean?
(*Check Day 32*)

G __ __  S __ __ __ __ __

Thank God for sending His perfect, loved Son to be your Saviour.

# DAY 38   TEMPTING TIMES

A plate of gooey, squidgy chocolate cakes, and no-one around. What do you do?
a) Snaffle one quickly while nobody's looking.
b) Wait patiently until tea time.
c) Scoff the lot!

The devil is sometimes called the tempter. He tempts us to do things which displease God—and is delighted when we give in. In today's reading, Jesus had nothing to eat for **40 days**. He was horribly hungry. Then the devil turned up with a tempting idea.

## READ
### Matthew 4v1-11

The devil tempted Jesus three times.
**Put the pictures in the right order.**

A- "Jump off the top"

B- "Worship me and I'll give you the world"

C- "Turn these stones into bread"

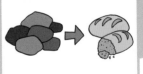

1 = \_\_\_ ,     2 = \_\_\_ ,     3 = \_\_\_

Did Jesus give in to the devil?  **YES / NO** \_\_\_\_\_

Jesus was **perfect**. He never sinned. Looking at Jesus helps us to see the right way to live.

## THINK + PRAY

The Bible promises that God will always help us when tempted. He will give us a way out. *This promise is in 1 Corinthians 10v13.*

Talk to God about this now. Ask Him to help you when tempted.

# DAY 39 KING'S KINGDOM

**xtb** Matthew 4v12-17

**Which one are you?** (Circle) one.

Walking wizard

Cycling sizzler

Skateboarding skidder

Running racer

## READ
### Matthew 4v12-13

Jesus walked miles—all over Israel.
Jesus moves around a lot in chapters 3 & 4.
**Draw His path on the map.**

From N _ _ _ _ _ _ _ (2v23) where Jesus grew up,

↓

Jordan river in J _ _ _ _ (3v1) where He was baptised,

↓

the d _ _ _ _ _ (4v1) where He was tempted,

↓

back to N _ _ _ _ _ _ _ (4v13)

↓

and finally to live in C _ _ _ _ _ _ _ _ _ (4v13).

## READ
### Matthew 4v17

Jesus didn't travel the country to go sight seeing! He had something very important to do. What was it?

_____

The kingdom of heaven is near because Jesus the King has arrived. People must **repent** (turn away from sin) and **follow Him** as King of their lives.

MAP OF ISRAEL
IN NEW TESTAMENT TIMES

**PRAY**
Ask Jesus the King to forgive you for disobeying Him, and to help you live your life with Him in charge.

# DAY 40 FOLLOW ME

**Spot the difference.**
There are eight to find.

## A FEW FOLLOWERS

### Read Matthew 4v18-22

Which four fishermen followed Jesus?

P_____     A_____

J_____     J_____

Their new job was to be "fishers of men". They didn't catch people in a net!—they told them all about Jesus the King. This was their job for the rest of their lives.

## LOTS OF FOLLOWERS

### Read Matthew 4v25

Crowds flocked to Jesus from a huge area.

 **Look again at yesterday's map to see where they came from.**
But sadly, later on in Matthew's book we see that many of these people turned their backs on Jesus.
They soon gave up.

## KEEP ON FOLLOWING

The four fishermen became **disciples**, which means "followers". They followed Jesus all their lives, even when it was difficult or dangerous.

## THINK SPOT

- Are **you** a follower of Jesus?
- Do you want to be? Go to **God's Rescue Plan** after Day 7 to find out more.
- Do you ever feel like giving up being a follower of Jesus?
- Do you want to tell your friends about Jesus?

**PRAY**   Talk to Jesus about your answers. Ask Him to help you.

# DAY 41   THE KING TEACHES

Jesus (the promised King) is telling people what it's like to follow Him—let's listen in!

**READ**
**Matthew 5v1-5**

Where was Jesus teaching? (v1)

Draw or write your answer here.

That's why it's called the **Sermon on the Mount** — heard of it?

*Take the first letter of each picture to find out about people who follow Jesus.*

**They are** _ _ _ _ _

Maybe your Bible says blessed or happy? Great! Jesus' followers are the happiest, luckiest people in the world! Why?

*Write down the red letters in order to find the answer.*

T_____ P_____ G____

---

**Verses 3-5** show us what the person who pleases God is like. *Draw a line to join each sentence with the right verse.*

Meek and humble, not proud of how good they are.    v3

Spiritually poor and depending on God, with nothing to offer Him.    v4

Sad because they disobey God.    v5

Surprised that it's not about being **good**? Check out lesson one!

**Lesson One**
Jesus' followers are the luckiest people in the world, because they know they need **God's help** to live His way.

**PRAY**   Dear God, please help me to realise that I need **Your** help to live **Your** way.

# DAY 42 WHAT ARE YOU DOING?

**What do you like doing?**
- ❏ Football
- ❏ TV
- ❏ Reading
- ❏ _____ your own

Add one of your own

### READ
**Matthew 5v6-9**

What does the person who follows Jesus **most** want to do?

What **G**_____ wants him to do. (v6)

Jesus' followers will be

**m**_____ (v7) and

**p**_____ in **h**_____ (v8)

and will work for

**p**_____ (v9).

---

Follow the lines to find out what each word means.

**merciful**

**pure in heart**

**working for peace**

Please God with all your choices, actions, likes and dislikes.

Forgive and be kind, even when it's hard or not fair.

Mend broken friendships.

**Need to change?**

Remember—God can help us **now**, AND **one day** He will make us perfect in heaven. Wow!

### READ
**Matthew 5v10-12**

Will following Jesus be easy or hard? _____

**Lesson Two** If you follow Jesus you will want to do what **God** wants you to do, even when it isn't easy.

Choose one of the red words

### PRAY

God, help me to be _____

by _____

_____ this week.

Decide how to put it into action

# DAY 43 MAKE A DIFFERENCE!

*Choose what would make a difference if you were:*

sick                                                salt

in a cave                                           water

thirsty                                             doctor

keeping food fresh without a fridge                 light

### READ
**Matthew 5v13-16**

People who follow Jesus make a **BIG** difference to the **WHOLE** world. How does Jesus describe them?

You are the s_____ of the earth (v13)

You are the l_____ of the world (v14)

---

But why does the world **need** salt and light?

The world needs **salt**

because it has rejected God. It is a dark place where people can't see what God is like or how to be rescued.

because it doesn't obey God. It is like meat rotting and going off – YUCK!

People who follow Jesus show a rotting world how God <u>does</u> want us to live.

The world needs **light**

*How can we live God's way? Look back at verses 3-12 to see.*

**What** will happen when we live the way God wants us to?

**People will p_____ our F_____ in h_____** (v16)

WOW!

**Lesson Three**
Living the way God wants us to will make a **BIG difference** to the world.

**PRAY**
Dear God, help me live the way You want, so that other people find out about You. Amen.

# DAY 44 SECRET NOT SHOWY!

**xtb** Matthew 6v1-4

Draw a picture of these things:

| | |
|---|---|
| toys | money |
| food | clothes |

These are all things that people give away to help others.

**READ**
**Matthew 6v1-4**

Jesus said that some people only give so that people will **praise** them. (v2)

**Does this please God?**  or

Crack the code to find out what sort of giving **pleases God** (v3,4)

___ ___ ___ ___ ___ ___

We need to talk to **some** people before we give something away—perhaps our parents. But we shouldn't boast about it—even to ourselves.

✔ *the thought bubble that would please God.*

> I hope everyone saw how much i gave.

> I hope my gift helps and that I don't show-off about it.

> I'm so generous!

**Lesson Four**  The person who follows Jesus gives things away to **please** God and **help** people, NOT to look good.

**THINK + PRAY**  Can you help someone today?  Who? _____
Ask God to help you do it without boasting.

# DAY 45 PLEASE GOD—NOT PEOPLE!

Cross out every **v**, **w** and **x** to find out what Jesus teaches us about next.

## xxwpwvxrvvxaxwvvxyxvwevvrxx

### READ
### Matthew 6v5-8

Why do some people pray?

*Use these words:* other  seen  people

**To be _____ by**

_____ (v5)

Is this the sort of prayer that pleases God?  ✔ or ✗ (v5 should help you)

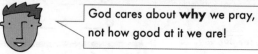

God cares about **why** we pray, not how good at it we are!

**Who** should we want to see us and be with us when we pray? (v6)

**Our**

F_____

**Praying is about talking to God, our Father.**

**Where** does Jesus say is a good place to pray? (v6)

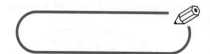

There's nothing magic about praying in your room! But it is a good place to pray. Find out why by following the arrows.

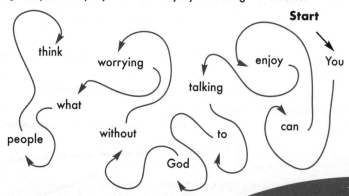

think    worrying    **Start**

enjoy    You

what    talking

can

people    without    to

God

**Lesson Five**  The person who follows Jesus prays because they love talking to God, NOT to look good.

**PRAY**  Thank God that we can always talk to Him.

# DAY 46 LONG WORDS OR LARGE PRAYERS?

Match the puzzle pieces to see what some people think praying is about:

Using many

Saying long

prayers

words

**READ**
Matthew 6v7-15

We don't have to use lots of long words—God is our Father and He loves us! He will give us everything we need. *Jesus taught His disciples this prayer:*

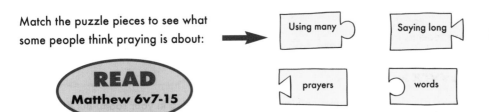

Our Father in heaven:
May your holy name be honoured;
may your kingdom come;
may your will be done on earth as it is in heaven.
Give us today our daily bread.
Forgive us the wrongs we have done, as we forgive the wrongs that others have done to us.
Do not bring us to a time of temptation, but keep us safe from the evil one.
                                        Amen

*This is called the Lord's Prayer*

Tell God how **holy** and amazing He is.

Ask for people to be saved into God's **kingdom**.

Ask for **God's will** to be done, not ours.

Ask for what you really **need**.

Ask God to **forgive** you for the wrongs you've done.

Ask God to **help** you not to do wrong.

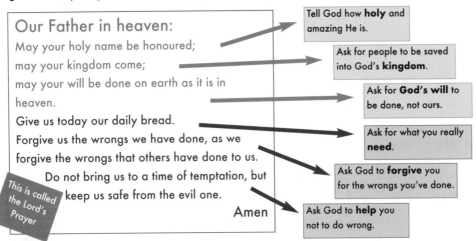

Did you notice that the first part (in red) is all about God? Jesus is showing us that we should put **God first** when we pray. Then we can pray LARGE prayers (for the things we really need, and for God's help).

**Find these words from the Lord's Prayer in the wordsearch**   honoured   will   kingdom   daily   temptation

| G | O | D | K | I | N | G | D | O | M |
| D | A | I | L | Y | F | I | R | S | T |
| T | E | M | P | T | A | T | I | O | N |
| U | S | H | O | N | O | U | R | E | D |
| W | I | L | L | S | E | C | O | N | D |

There should be **four** words left over. They tell us how we should pray...

G _ _   F _ _ _ _ _

U _   S _ _ _ _ _ _

**Lesson Six**  You can pray LARGE prayers without using long words.

**PRAY**

Read verses 9-13 aloud as a prayer.

# DAY 47  WHAT DO YOU WANT?

Follow the lines to find out what these people want.

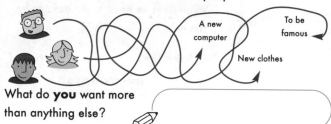

A new computer

To be famous

New clothes

What do **you** want more than anything else?

Jesus calls these things our **treasures**.

### READ
**Matthew 6v19-21**

What's the problem with storing things up on earth?

stolen ← and ← destroyed ← get ← They

**Things on earth don't last—so they don't make good treasures!**

<u>Where</u> does treasure last for ever? (v20) **H_____**

**Pleasing God** and **following Jesus** is like putting treasure into a box in heaven where we can enjoy it for ever. That's the treasure we should really want!

### READ
**Matthew 6v31-34**

Should we worry about the things we need, like food and clothes? (v31)

 ✔ or ✗

Who can we trust to look after us? (v32)
**Our F_____ in heaven.**

So don't let the everyday things you need take all your attention. *Shade in the coins with **A**, **B** or **C** on them to find out what should be most important to us.*

**Lesson Seven**    Trust God and put Him first.

**THINK + PRAY**    Think of the things that are more important to you than God. Ask Him to help you to put Him first.

# DAY 48 DON'T JUDGE

Circle the things this **tennis** player has got wrong.

Jesus says we're good at spotting wrong things others do, but rubbish at spotting the ways **we** disobey God!

## READ
## Matthew 7v1-5

What does Jesus tells us **not** to do?(v1)

Do not **J_____** others.

---

So we shouldn't be nasty, or pleased when someone does something wrong.

AND we must remember that:

*Put the spaces between words in the right places*

**Wedi sobe yGo dtoo.**

W__ d_____ G____ t___

Think about the person in verse 3. What **does** he notice?
☐ The plank/log in his own eye
☐ The speck in his friend/brother's eye

---

What does he need to do **before** he can help his friend? (v5)

**Take the** _____ **out of his own eye.**

It's good to help others obey God, but **first** ask God to forgive you and help you to obey Him.

**Lesson Eight**
Don't judge your friends; remember your own disobedience, and God's forgiveness.

**PRAY**

Dear God, help me not to think I'm better than my friends. Help me to remember that You have forgiven me loads. Amen

# DAY 49 GET HELP!

*Sermon on the Mount*

I'm really excited about following Jesus! But there's a lot I need to change after reading the **Sermon on the Mount**.

Today Jesus teaches about **asking God to help us follow Him**.

## READ Matthew 7v7-8

Link up the puzzle pieces to see what Jesus promises in v7.

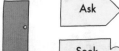

| | |
|---|---|
| Ask | Knock |
| find | |
| Seek | door will open |
| receive | |

## READ Matthew 7v9-11

What are the **good** things the child asks for? (v9, 10)

What are the **harmful** things the father could give the child? (v9,10)

Draw or write your answers in the boxes

Does the father give **good** things or **harmful** things? (v11)

**IF** a **human father**
...who is **not perfect**
...gives **good** gifts to his children;

**THEN** we can know for sure
that **God**
...who is **perfect**
...will give us **good** things when we ask.

*Unravel the word in the speech bubble to find out the best thing we can ask God for.*

l e h p

H_____ to follow Him.

**Lesson Nine** Keep asking God to help you to follow Him.

## PRAY

Dear God, thank you that You will always help me follow You.

# DAY 50 CHOOSE WISELY

What choices do you make?

☐ What to wear
☐ Who to talk to
☐ What to read

Add one of your own

_____

Our **biggest** choice is whether we will obey Jesus or not.

## READ
### Matthew 7v24-29

*Draw a line from the people to show what they did when they heard Jesus.*

Person 1
(v24)

Person 2
(v26)

Didn't do what Jesus said

Obeyed Jesus

---

What are we like if we **obey** Jesus? (v24)

**A w_____ person who built his h_____ on r_____**

*What happens to that house in the storm? (v25)*

Draw or write your answer

What are we like if we **disobey** Jesus? (v26)

**A f_____ person who built his h_____ on s_____**

*What happens to that house in the storm? (v27)*

Draw or write your answer

---

**Lesson Ten**

If we choose to obey Jesus, we are like the house on the rock. We will keep going when it is hard and we will be with Jesus in heaven when we die.

*Sermon on the Mount*

**Wow!** What a lot we've learned from the

Look back at all ten lessons. Does it seem hard to live God's way? Ask Him to help you!

**THINK + PRAY**

Think of the times you hear Jesus' teaching (*in church, reading the Bible, in XTB...*) Ask God to help you obey it and not just hear it.

# DAY 51 MEET THE FAMILY

Welcome back to the book of **GENESIS**—The Book of **Beginnings**.
The next part of Genesis is about the beginnings of God's special people, the Israelites.
We begin with just three people...

**ABRAM**
(later called Abraham)
• 75 years old
• The Bible calls Abram a **friend of God**.
• We'll find out why—and how **we** can be God's friends too.

**SARAI**
(later called Sarah)
• Abram's wife
• 65 years old
• Has never been able to have children—and now she's too old.

**LOT**
• Abram's nephew
• Lot's father died, so he lives with Abram and Sarai.
• Good at getting into trouble!

As we catch up with them, the family have already travelled a l-o-n-g way. They left the city of **Ur**, and travelled hundreds of miles to **Haran**.

**?** 4000 years ago there were no cars or aeroplanes. How do you think they got there?

Abram's father Terah was with them then, but he was very old. He died in Haran.

Soon it will be time for the family to set off for another country...

God was about to make some incredible promises to Abram. *Use the arrow code to find out what they were.*

**1**

**2**

**3**

Look for these three promises as you read the Bible story.

## READ
### Genesis 12v1-9

What amazing promises from God!

**Stick a Promise sticker here** ➡

**ARROW**

**CODE**

⇧ = A

⬈ = B

⇨ = C

⬂ = D

⇩ = E

⇦ = G

⬃ = H

⬆ = I

⬀ = J

⬋ = L

⬊ = N

◁ = R

▷ = S

### Think Spot

God told Abram to leave his home, his father's family and his country. Do you think it was easy for Abram to leave this all behind?

Draw Abram's journey on the map. *Draw a line starting at UR, up to HARAN then down to CANAAN.*

**THINK + PRAY**

Abram left everything he knew behind him—and he didn't even know where he was going! Why do you think Abram trusted God so much? Ask God to help **you** to trust Him as much as Abram did.

# DAY 52 TO AND FRO? YES AND NO!

xtb Genesis 12v10-20

**WORD POOL**

 YES  NO  NO!  YES  NO  YES  YES

Loads of 'toing and 'froing today (and yes-ing and no-ing!) *Use the word pool to check your answers, by matching the shape and colour of each box.*

In yesterday's story, did Abram go to the land God told him to go to?

Did God promise to **bless** Abram in this new land?

But it looks like Abram was finding it hard to **keep** trusting God...

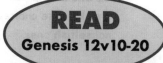
## READ
### Genesis 12v10-20

The famine meant there was very little food to eat. So Abram left Canaan and went to **Egypt** instead. (*Draw his journey on yesterday's map.*)

Did Abram ask **God** if he should go to Egypt? (v10)

Sarai was very beautiful. Abram was worried that the king of Egypt (called Pharaoh) would kill Abram so that he could marry Sarai. So Abram told Sarai to pretend to be his **sister**.

Was Sarai really Abram's sister? ⬭ and ⬡

Actually this was a **half-truth**—because Sarai was Abram's **half-sister**. But she was also his **wife**!

**What a mess!**
Abram and Sarai told lies. So the king took Sarai to live in his palace, because he thought she was unmarried. **But God sorted it all out.** He showed the king who Sarai really was—and the king sent Abram and Sarai back to Canaan where they belonged. (*Draw their journey home on yesterday's map.*)

## THINK + PRAY

Did Abram let God down in this story?

Did God let Abram down?
We **all** let God down sometimes—but God **never** lets us down! Thank God that He is like this.

# DAY 53 WHAT A LOT!

What a lot of sheep! Can you spot the odd one out?

Abram, Sarai and Lot have come back from Egypt. But there's a problem. Too many sheep!

(and goats... and cows... and...)

There won't be enough food and water if they all stay together. So Abram decides it will be better if he and Lot split up.

## READ
### Genesis 13v8-13

---

Abram had the right to make the first choice—but who did he give the choice to instead? (v11) **L_____**

### Lot had two choices:

**A** The beautiful Jordan valley. Plenty of green grass and fresh water for his flocks. But close to the **evil** city of Sodom.

**B** The hills of Canaan. Harder to farm—but well away from Sodom and the wicked people who live there.

Did Lot choose **A** or **B**? _____ (v11)

*Oh No!*

Lot pitched his tents close to Sodom. His selfish choice was very foolish, as we'll see in chapter 14.

---

### Think Spot

Followers of Jesus need to ask God to help them to make wise choices.

For example, Dave has been friends with Jon and Pete for ages. But now they've started stealing stuff. As a follower of Jesus what should Dave do?

What would **you** do?

## PRAY
Ask God to help you to make **wise** choices—not **selfish** ones.

# DAY 54 A DUSTY PROMISE?

 Genesis 13v14-18

Follow the compass directions to spell the mystery word. **Start** in the bottom left hand corner. **Move** 4 squares East; then 5 squares North; 4 squares East; 3 squares South; 2 squares West

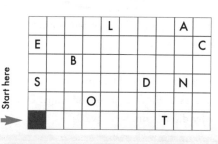

Every time you land on a letter, copy it here.

_ _ _ _ _

Abram and Lot have just split the land between them. Lot chose the green valley to farm in. Abram was left with the hills. It looks like Abram has lost out—but see what God promises him...

**READ** Genesis 13v14-18

Which directions did God tell Abram to look? (v14)

How much of the land does God promise Abram? (v15)

Can you count all the **dots** in this box? Maybe you can—if you're very careful—but imagine trying to count all the **dust** on the earth! God says that counting Abram's family will be as hard as this!

 At first it looked like Abram had lost out when the land was split. But God's promises to him were far more valuable than a field for his sheep!

**Stick a Promise sticker here** ➡️

**THINK + PRAY** Look out of your window (or go outside if you can). Look as far as you can in every direction. God's promises to Abram were **H-U-G-E**! God gives **us** huge promises too. He promises to love us, to listen when we pray and to be with us all the time. Thank God for His huge promises to you.

# DAY 55 THE BATTLE OF THE KINGS

 Genesis 14v1-20

Remember Lot's foolish choice to live near the wicked city of Sodom? Now he's moved right inside the city itself—and it's a very dangerous place to be!

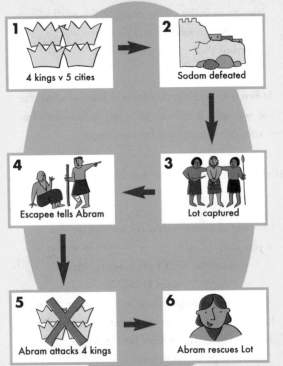

1 — 4 kings v 5 cities
2 — Sodom defeated
3 — Lot captured
4 — Escapee tells Abram
5 — Abram attacks 4 kings
6 — Abram rescues Lot

**1** Four powerful kings attacked the five cities in the Jordan valley (including Sodom).

**2** Sodom was defeated.

**3** Everyone from Sodom was captured, including Lot and his family.

**4** One man escaped, and rushed off to find Abram.

**5** Abram called his men together, attacked the four kings—and won!

**6** Abram brought Lot and his family back.

## READ
### Genesis 14v14-20

How many fighting men did Abram have? (v14) _____

That was nothing like enough to beat the armies of the four powerful kings! So why did Abram win? (v20)

**Because _____ gave him victory.**

 **WOW!** It looked impossible—but God was on Abram's side. No contest!!!

**PRAY** Are you worried about anything at the moment? **Nothing** is too difficult for God. Ask Him to help you.

# DAY 56 MEET MELCHIZEDEK

Genesis 14v17-24

Abram had rescued Lot—along with all the other people from Sodom, and their belongings. Usually the reward for winning a battle was to keep everything (and everyone!) you captured. So what would Abram do?

**READ**
**Genesis 14v17-24**

Circle the right words:

After the battle, Abram came back to the **forest / Jordan valley / tower of London**. He was met by **2 / 3 / 4** kings. Melchizedek was a priest. He was also king of **Salem / Seattle / Sydney**. Melchizedek gave Abram bread and **milk / cola / wine**, and he blessed Abram. Abram gave him **a bit / a tenth / none** of everything he brought back. The **queen / king / prince** of Sodom wanted Abram to keep some of the loot from Sodom. But Abram refused to keep even a **buckle / button / thread!**

**NOTHING from Sodom**
Abram didn't want his wealth to come from such an evil king. (v23) Abram knew that **God** would provide for all his needs.

**EVERYTHING from God**
Abram knew that everything he had came from **God**. He gave a tenth back to God, by giving it to God's priest, Melchizedek. (v20)

**THINK + PRAY**
Everything **you** have comes from God. What can you give back to Him? (Your love? Your time? Your...?) Talk to God about your answers.

*Did you know?*
The New Testament says that Melchizedek points us to the only perfect King and Priest—**JESUS**.

# DAY 57 SEEING STARS

A sky full of stars—but only one is identical to the one on the right. Which one?

Abram was worried because he and Sarai still didn't have any children. It looked like one of Abram's **servants** would inherit everything...

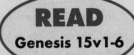

**READ**
Genesis 15v1-6

---

Abram and Sarai were really **old** by now. Abram thought his servant would inherit everything from him. But what did God promise Abram? (v4)

What did God tell Abram to look at? (v5)

I once stayed in a cottage in Scotland. No street lights. A clear night. **Stunning stars!** I'd never seen so many in my life. That's how it would have been for Abram too.

---

God's promise was incredible—and Abram **believed** Him (v6).

**Time for another Promise sticker.**

**Think Spot**
Genesis tells us that God is the **Star-Maker**. The very same God who made the stars in the first place was making this promise to Abram and Sarai. Do you think God was able to keep His promise? Why?

**PRAY**
When you pray, you are talking to God the Star-Maker. How does that make you feel? Talk to God about it.

# DAY 58 GOD'S FRIENDS

 How can I be God's friend?

What would you say to Philip?

The Bible calls Abram a **friend of God** (James 2v23). But we know that Abram **sinned**—and that sin **stops** people from being God's friends. So **why** was Abram called God's friend? *Today's reading shows us the answer.*

## READ
### Genesis 15v6

*Fill in the missing vowels:*

☆=a; ★=e; ✪=i; ✹=o; ☆=u

f r ✪ ★ n d
_ _ _ _ _ _

b ★ l ✪ ★ v ★ d
_ _ _ _ _ _ _ _

t r ☆ s t ★ d
_ _ _ _ _ _ _

 ☆ b r ☆ m
_ _ _ _ _

r ✪ g h t ★ ✹ ☆ s
_ _ _ _ _ _ _ _ _

**Did you know?**
Being **righteous** means being **right with God**.

Abram **believed** God—and God accepted him. Abram didn't have to keep lots of rules, or live a perfect life. He **trusted** God's promises—and that made him **right with God**. He was God's friend.

*Sounds familiar? If you're not sure why, have a quick peek at **Am I a Christian?** before Day 8.*

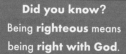 **THINK + PRAY**

Are **you** a friend of God? Check out the prayer at the end of **Am I a Christian?**. If you've prayed that prayer, or one like it, and really meant it, then you are a friend of God too. Thank God for sending Jesus so that you can become His friend.

A **covenant** is an agreement that mustn't be broken. Abram needed to be sure God would keep His promises about the land of Canaan. So God made a **covenant** with Abram.

### Did You Know?

When people made covenants in those days, they'd kill some animals or birds, then walk between the dead bodies! That's what v7-11 and v17-21 are all about.

After Abram had brought the animals and birds, God made him fall into a deep sleep. Then He told Abram what would happen to him and his family in the future…

## READ
### Genesis 15v12-16

Draw a line between each promise and it's answer.

**What God said:**

"Your family will be slaves for 400 years." (v13)

"You, Abram, will die in peace at a good old age." (v15)

"Your family will be rescued and return to Canaan." (v16)

**What happened:**

Abram died peacefully when he was 175 years old. (Genesis 25v7-8)

The Israelites (Abram's family) were slaves in Egypt for 400 years. (Exodus 2v23-24)

God chose Moses to lead the Israelites out of Egypt. (Exodus 3v15-17)

If you want to find out more, read the Bible verses.

## THINK + PRAY

All the way through the Bible we see that God is a **Promise-Giver** and a **Promise-Keeper**.

**Stick a Promise sticker here.** ➡

PROMISE

God **never** makes promises that He can't keep! Thank Him for being like this.

# DAY 60 WAITING FOR GOD

Sally didn't want to wait for her dad to mend her bike. She tried to fix it herself—rode it—and what do you think happened?

Abram and Sarai waited **10 years** for God to give them a son. Then they decided to fix the problem themselves.

## READ
### Genesis 16v1-2

Sarai told Abram to take her servant Hagar as his second wife. That way Abram could have a son. Abram agreed, but after Hagar became pregnant, she began to look down on Sarai. Then Sarai started to treat Hagar badly—so Hagar ran away.

## READ
### Genesis 16v7-10

Use these words to fill in the gaps.

back    away    huge

I'm running _____. (v8)

Go _____ to your mistress. (v9)

You will have a _____ family. (v10)

So Hagar went back to Abram and Sarai as God had told her. Later she gave birth to a son, who was called **Ishmael**.

## Did you know?

God kept His promise to Hagar. Ishmael was the start of a h-u-g-e family.

But he **wasn't** the son God had promised to Abram and Sarai. They still had to wait much longer before their son was born.

## THINK + PRAY

Sometimes it's very hard to trust that God will do what's best for us. Instead, we want to make things happen on our own. Can you think of times like that? Ask God to help you to trust Him, and to wait patiently.

# DAY 61 NEW NAMES

If you could change your name to anything you like, what would it be?

_____

Imagine changing your name when you're 99! That's how old Abram was when God gave him a new name...

## READ
## Genesis 17v1-8

What does **Abraham** mean?

_Cross out the x's:_

XFXAATXHXEXRX XOXFX XMXAAXNXY

_ _ _ _ _ _ _ _ _ _ _ _ _ _

**TRUE TALE:** My friend wanted everyone to know how **happy** she was to be a follower of Jesus. So she changed her name from Joyce to **Joy**!

---

Have you noticed how every time God told Abraham about His **covenant** , Abraham learnt a bit more...?

Some of your family will be XKXIXNXGXSX.

_ _ _ _ _ _

I will be XTXHXEXIXRX XGXOXDX

_ _ _ _ _   _ _ _

Then God told Abraham that he and his family were to be **circumcised** (a small piece of skin cut off). This would be a **sign** of God's covenant promises to them.

## READ  Genesis 17v15

Sarai was given a new name as well. What was it? **S_____**

---

God told Abraham that he and Sarah were soon to have a son, called **Isaac**. When did God say that Isaac would be born? (See v21)

_____

As soon as God stopped speaking to Abraham, he and his family were all circumcised, just as God had said.

**THINK + PRAY**

Read verse 1 again. God told Abraham to "**walk before Him**". This meant to live his life looking to God, obeying and trusting Him. Do you want to obey and trust God like Abraham?

If so, tell God, and ask Him to help you.

# DAY 62 THREE STRANGERS

Imagine you're watching your fave TV show—and the doorbell rings. You open the door—and can't believe your eyes! It's

_____

← *Who would you like it to be?*

In today's reading, some visitors turn up at Abraham's front door. (Of his tent!) One of them was **God**!

## READ
### Genesis 18v1-2

How many men came to see Abraham?

As Abraham soon realised, one of His visitors was God. The other two were angels. Abraham ran to make them a special meal. Then he waited nearby, under a tree.

## READ
### Genesis 18v9-15

What did God say would happen in a year's time? (v10)

_____

**Time for another Promise sticker** ➡  PROMISE

Sarah was inside the tent, listening. What did she do? (v12)

> **She**
> I_____

Sarah knew she was far too **old** to have a baby. But God reminded her that He can do **anything**. (v14)

## THINK + PRAY

God knew what Sarah was thinking—even when she tried to lie about it. God knows everything **we** think and say and do—even when no-one else does. Is there anything you need to say sorry to God about? Ask Him to forgive you, and to help you to trust and obey Him.

# DAY 63 A SON IS BORN

Crack the code as a reminder of God's words to Abraham.

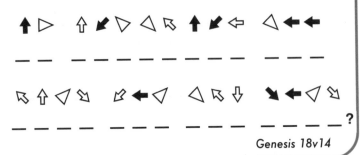

_____ _____ _____ _____ _____ _____ _____ _____ _____ _____

_____ _____ _____ _____ _____ _____ _____ _____ _____ _____

_____ _____ _____ _____ _____ _____ _____ _____ _____?

*Genesis 18v14*

**The answer is NO!**

Nothing is impossible for God the Star-Maker. We're skipping ahead a few chapters to see how God kept His promise to give a son to a 90 year old woman.

## READ
### Genesis 21v1-7

Did God keep His promise to Abraham and Sarah?

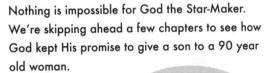

Stick your last Promise sticker here ➡

**ARROW**
**CODE**

⇑ = A
⇲ = D
⇓ = E
↯ = F
⇐ = G
↘ = H
↑ = I
↘ = L
↙ = N
← = O
◁ = R
▷ = S
◁ = T
▽ = U
▷ = Y

Abraham and Sarah called their son **Isaac**. What does this name mean?

_____ _____ _____ _____ _____ _____ _____ _____

Yesterday we saw how Sarah laughed when God said she would have a baby at such an old age. Abraham had laughed at the idea too. (Genesis 17v17) But now this old couple were laughing for **joy**!

**THINK + PRAY**

Sarah laughed with delight because God had kept His promise to her. Are **you** excited that God is the Promise-Keeper? How can you use **your voice** to show Him your joy? (praying, singing, laughing, telling someone else about Him...) Choose **one** way to thank God for keeping all His promises.

# DAY 64 THE TOUGHEST TEST

**xtb** Genesis 22v1-14

## READ
### Genesis 22v1-2

What does verse 1 say that God did?

**God**
t_____
**Abraham.**

It was a very hard test. Hard for **Abraham** to do. Hard for **us** to understand.

*Did you know?*

**SACRIFICES**
Abraham would be used to making sacrifices. He would kill an animal or bird, burn it, and offer it to God. It was a way of saying sorry or thank you to God. But this time God told Abraham to sacrifice his own **son**!

---

Use these words to fill in the gaps.

three          obeyed
         loved
   mountain          knife

Isaac was now growing up. Abraham l_____ his son very much. But who did Abraham love **most**? His son? Or God? That was the test. When God told Abraham to take Isaac to a m_____ in the land of Moriah, he o_____ straight away. It took t_____ days to get there. Then Abraham took his son, put him on top of the wood and lifted his k_____ ready to kill Isaac.

## READ
### Genesis 22v9-14

---

**Wow!** Abraham really was going to kill his son! He showed that he loved God more than anything or anyone else. But God **stopped** Abraham.

What did God provide instead?
**A r_____** (v13)
The ram died in Isaac's place.

## THINK + PRAY

The Bible says we should love God **more** than anything or anyone else. This doesn't mean that you stop loving your family and friends. In fact, God will help you to love them even more than you do now! But it does mean that God is the most important person in your life. Do you want to love God this much? Then ask Him to help you.

# DAY 65 SUBSTITUTE

### A SUBSTITUTE PLAYER
Steve was in the school team. But he hurt his ankle and had to stop playing. Phil was the **substitute** that day. He came on in Steve's place.

### A SUBSTITUTE SACRIFICE
Yesterday we saw that Abraham loved God more than anything. He was willing to **sacrifice** his own son. But God provided a substitute. A ram died in Isaac's **place**.

### A SUBSTITUTE FOR US
**"The Lamb of God, who takes away the <u>sin</u> of the world." John 1v29**

Who was **John** the Baptist talking about? *To find out, fit the <u>underlined</u> words into the puzzle.*

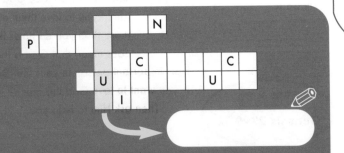

**xtb** Genesis 22v15-19

## READ
### Genesis 22v15-19

**"Through your offspring all nations on earth will be blessed." (v18)**

### It's JESUS!
- **Jesus** came from Abraham's family. He was born 2000 years after Abraham.
- **Jesus** was just like a lamb to be sacrificed. He died in our place, to take the punishment for our sins.
- This is how **Jesus** was God's way of blessing the whole world.

### THINK + PRAY
God kept His promise to Abraham by sending His own Son Jesus to be our **substitute**. Jesus died in our place, so that we can be forgiven. Are you thankful to God for sending Jesus as your substitute? Talk to Him about it now.

**Want to know more?**
For a free booklet called **Why did Jesus die?** write to us at XTB, The Good Book Company, Blenheim House, 1 Blenheim Road, Epsom, Surrey, KT19 9AP, UK   Or email us: alison@thegoodbook.co.uk

# TIME FOR MORE?

Have you read all 65 days of XTB?
Well done if you have!

How often do you use XTB?
- Every day?
- Nearly every day?
- Two or three times a week?
- Now and then?

XTB comes out every three months. If you've been using it every day, or nearly every day, that's great! You may still have a few weeks to wait before you get the next issue of XTB. But don't worry!—that's what the extra readings are for...

## XTB TIME

**When do <u>you</u> read XTB?**

In the morning.

When I get back from school.

At bedtime.

## EXTRA READINGS
The next four pages contain some extra Bible readings to help you find out more about what God is like. If you read one each day, they will take you 26 days. Or you may want to read two or three each day. Or just pick a few to try. Whichever suits you best. There's a cracking wordsearch to solve too...

*The extra readings start on the next page*

# WHAT'S GOD LIKE?

The book of Genesis has helped us to find out what God is like. In these extra readings we're going to see what some other parts of the Bible say about God's character.

The ideas in the box will help you...

---

**PRAY**   Ask God to help you to understand what you read.

**READ**   Read the Bible verses, and fill in the missing word in the puzzle.

**THINK**   Think about what you have just read.

**PRAY**   Thank God for what you have learned about Him.

---

There are 26 Bible readings on the next three pages. Part of each verse has been printed for you—but with a word missing. Fill in the missing words as you read the verses. Then see if you can find them all in the wordsearch below. Some are written backwards—or diagonally!

*If you get stuck, check the answers at the end of Reading 26.*

| M | S | N | N | D | M | S | S | I | C | H | A | N | G | E |
|---|---|---|---|---|---|---|---|---|---|---|---|---|---|---|
| E | N | S | E | G | Y | P | T | V | D | O | O | G | C | S |
| R | O | A | D | X | S | R | E | H | T | O | M | A | D | O |
| C | T | E | T | R | V | E | S | E | G | R | F | R | V | S |
| Y | H | B | D | F | O | S | H | F | T | U | O | S | I | C |
| F | I | R | E | A | A | W | E | R | O | W | O | N | D | A |
| Y | N | H | E | A | R | T | P | V | S | R | N | H | O | R |
| T | G | S | E | H | N | K | H | T | E | E | G | B | T | E |
| H | P | R | O | M | I | S | E | E | R | I | B | I | V | R |
| G | L | O | R | Y | A | A | R | S | R | T | L | I | V | S |
| R | G | R | S | S | R | N | D | G | O | D | S | E | R | E |
| E | V | O | L | S | S | E | N | D | O | O | G | S | B | B |

**1** ☐ **Read Exodus 20v1-6**

God reminded the Israelites of all that He had done for them.

"I am the LORD your God who brought you out of E _ _ _ _ where you were slaves." (v2)

**2** ☐ **Read Deuteronomy 4v23-24**

Moses warned the Israelites not to follow pretend gods.

"The Lord your God is like a flaming f _ _ _ ." (v24)

**3** ☐ **Read Deuteronomy 10v17-22**

Moses reminded the Israelites that God is fair and just.

"God does not show partiality, and he does not accept b _ _ _ _ _ ."
(v17)

**4** ☐ **Read Joshua 23v14-16**

Joshua reminded the Israelites that God keep His promises.

"Every p _ _ _ _ _ _ God made has been kept; not one has failed."
(v14)

**5** ☐ **Read 1 Samuel 16v6-7**

God told Samuel what kind of king He was looking for.

"Man looks at the outward appearance, but God looks at the
h _ _ _ _ ." (v7)

**6** ☐ **Read 1 Samuel 17v41-47**

David told Goliath why God would help him to beat the huge Philistine.

"The whole world will know that Israel has a God, and everyone here will see that the LORD does not need
s _ _ _ _ _ _ or spears to save his people." (v46-47)

**7** ☐ **Read Psalm 19v1-6**

Psalm 19 shows how the world points us to God our Creator.

"How clearly the sky reveals God's
g _ _ _ _ ." (v1)

**8** ☐ **Read Psalm 23v1-4**

David (who was a shepherd himself) wrote a song about God being a shepherd too.

"The LORD is my
s _ _ _ _ _ _ _ _ :
I have everything I need." (v1)

**9** ☐ **Read Psalm 23v5-6**

The second half of David's song about God our Shepherd...

"I know that your
g _ _ _ _ _ _ _ _ and love will be with me all my life." (v6)

**10** ☐ **Read Psalm 33v1-5**
This psalm shows that what God says always comes true.
"The W _ _ _ _ of the LORD are true and all his works are dependable." (v4)

**11** ☐ **Read Psalm 51v1-9**
David's song about God's compassion and mercy.
"Have m _ _ _ _ on me, O God, because of your constant love. Because of your great mercy wipe away my sins!" (v1)

**12** ☐ **Read Psalm 65v9-13**
David writes about how God looks after our world.
"You show your C _ _ _ for the land by sending rain; you make it rich and fertile." (v9)

**13** ☐ **Read Psalm 106v1-3**
A long psalm, thanking God for His goodness to the Israelites.
"Give thanks to the LORD, because he is g _ _ _ ; his love is eternal."(v1)

**14** ☐ **Read Psalm 139v1-6**
This psalm shows us how much God knows about us.
"You know everything I do; from far away you understand all my t _ _ _ _ _ _ _ ." (v2)

**15** ☐ **Read Psalm 139v7-12**
Everywhere we go, God can see us and help us.
"Even darkness is not d _ _ _ for you." (v12)

**16** ☐ **Read Psalm 139v13-18**
God knew all about you before you were even born!
"You created every part of me; you put me together in my m _ _ _ _ _ ' _ womb." (v13)

**17** ☐ **Read Isaiah 40v25-26**
Isaiah reminds his readers that God is the one who made and knows each star.
"He calls each star by n _ _ _ ." (v26)

**18** ☐ **Read Malachi 3v6**
Malachi (the last book in the Old Testament) tells us that God always stays the same.
"I am the LORD, and I do not c _ _ _ _ _ ." (v6)

## 19 ☐ Read Luke 1v35-38

*The angel Gabriel tells Mary that God can do anything.*

"For n _ _ _ _ _ _ is impossible with God—there is nothing that God cannot do." (v37)

## 20 ☐ Read John 3v16-17

*John tells us why God sent His Son Jesus to die for us.*

"For God loved the world so much that he gave his only Son, so that everyone who b _ _ _ _ _ _ _ _ in him may not die but have eternal life." (v16)

## 21 ☐ Read John 14v8-11

*Philip asked Jesus to show him what God is like. Jesus said:*

"Whoever has seen me has seen the F _ _ _ _ _ _." (v9)

## 22 ☐ Read Romans 5v6-11

*Paul's letter to Christians in Rome shows us how much God loves us.*

"But God has shown us how much he loves us—it was while we were still s _ _ _ _ _ _ _ that Christ died for us!" (v8)

## 23 ☐ Read 1 John 1v8-10

*John reminds us that we sin—and need to ask God to forgive us.*

"If we confess our sins to God ... he will f _ _ _ _ _ _ us our sins." (v9)

## 24 ☐ Read 1 John 4v7-10

*John goes on to say that we know that God loves us because He sent Jesus to die for us.*

"God is l _ _ _." (v8)

## 25 ☐ Read Revelation 21v1-4

*The book of Revelation ends with a picture of what heaven will be like.*

"God will wipe away all t _ _ _ _ from their eyes. There will be no more death, no more grief or crying or pain." (v4)

## 26 ☐ Read Revelation 21v22-27

*Heaven is like a city—with no need for sun or moon because God is its light.*

"The city has no need of the sun or the moon to shine on it, because the glory of G _ _ shines on it, and the Lamb is its lamp." (v23)

# WHAT NEXT?

XTB comes out every three months.
Each issue contains 65 full XTB pages, plus
26 days of extra readings. By the time
you've used them all, the next issue of XTB
will be available.

## ISSUE TWO: *Miracles and Dreams*

Issue Two of XTB carries on in the books of Genesis, Matthew
and Acts. It dips into the book of Psalms as well.

- Meet Jacob the Schemer and Joseph the Dreamer in the
  book of **Genesis**.
- Investigate Jesus' miracles in **Matthew's** Gospel.
- Discover why Peter's dream changed everything for the
  first Christians as you read more of the book of **Acts**.

**Issue Two of XTB comes with masses of codes to crack!**

Available from your local Good Book
Company website:
UK: www.thegoodbook.co.uk
North America: www.the goodbook.com
Australia: www.thegoodbook.com.au
New Zealand: www.thegoodbook.co.nz

## Look out for these special seasonal editions of XTB!

### Christmas Unpacked

Three weeks of Bible readings to help you focus on
what Christmas is really all about. Meet Dr. Luke
as he tells you all about God's Rescue Plan.
Find out WHO the Rescuer is and WHY we need
rescuing. *Comes with free Rescue stickers.*

### Easter Unscrambled

Unscramble the meaning of Easter with the help of
Dr. Luke. Discover what the last part of Luke's book
tells us about Who Jesus is and Why He came.
*Comes with free Rescue stickers.*

### Summer Signposts

A three week Summer Expedition to discover the
real Jesus. Zoom in on the seven signposts from
John's book about Jesus. Follow the clues to
discover Who Jesus is and Why He came. *Comes
with a free magnifying glass.*

### Do you know any good jokes?
—send them in and they might appear in XTB!

### Do you have any questions?
...about anything you've read in XTB.
—send them in and we'll do our best to answer them.

**Write to:** XTB, The Good Book Company, Blenheim House, 1 Blenheim Road, Epsom,
Surrey, KT19 9AP, UK **or e-mail me:** alison@thegoodbook.co.uk